Return to KANSAS

Return to KANSAS

watercolors by J.R. Hamil

text by
Sharon Hamil

SOUTHWIND PRESS

Second Printing

©Copyright 1984 by Southwind Press, Inc.
All Rights Reserved
Printed in the United States of America
Library of Congress Catalog Card Number: 84-51557

Distributed by University Press of Kansas
303 Carruth, Lawrence, Kansas 66045 USA
Printed by Vile-Goller/Fine Arts Printing & Lithographing
Kansas City, Kansas USA
Color by Corona Litho
Kansas City, Missouri USA

"We need writers and artists to proclaim the beauty of Kansas..."

Karl Menninger in 1939

Front end sheets: *"Flint Hills Wildflowers" east of Marion.*

Frontispiece: *These windmills on the prairie bring life-giving water to the cattle grazing the Flint Hills.*

Cottonwood trees grow tall along the Missouri River in Doniphan County near White Cloud. It's probably a place like this one where God rested one day before finishing the rest of his work on Kansas.

RETURN TO KANSAS presents images of the state as it is today, firmly rooted in the Kansas past. Through the artist's eye you see the beauty of the Kansas sky, the sweep of uninterrupted horizons, the splendor of golden wheat fields, the grandeur of the Flint Hills, the serenity of grazing cattle, and the myriad other things which are distinctly Kansas.

Kansas offers tremendous variety. Ours is a state of wheat and cattle, oil and gas, airplane production and other industries... a land steeped in history, the history of soldiers and forts, homesteaders and wagon trains, Indian conflicts and treaties, cowboys and cattle drives, trade on the Santa Fe Trail, and mail delivery by Pony Express. The strength and perseverance of Kansas and its people seem to reflect the optimism born in those early days. As William Allen White said, "Kansas is Kansas largely because of the people who came here."

"Cows in Winter" north of Lecompton.

In creating RETURN TO KANSAS, we received much help and would like to express our thanks... to the investors who made the funding possible, to Pat Spillman for editing, to Rob McKnight for his witty captions, and to Fred Woodward and staff at the University Press of Kansas. Research materials were provided by the Kansas Department of Economic Development, the Kansas Historical Society, the Johnson County Public Library, the office of Secretary of State Jack Brier and the many individuals who told us of backroads, treasured favorite places, and who gave us glimpses into their lives.

We hope that, when you close the book, images will remain that will intensify your appreciation for the beauty of Kansas.

Sharon and Jim Hamil

"Farm Pond Boat"

Contents

THE LAY OF THE LAND
topography, archeology, and geography 2

THE KAW AND ITS COMPANIONS
rivers and other waters 7

THE FIRST KANSANS
tribes and troubles 14

MANY BACKGROUNDS
ethnic mixing, homesteading, and worshiping 23

WELL WORN PATHS
trails, cattle drives, railroads 32

GIFTS FROM THE LAND
wheat, sorghum, corn, soybeans 42

INDUSTRY THRIVES
minerals and manufacturing 61

KANSAS CULTURE
learning, governing, healing, and relaxing 71

For almost 400 miles along I-70 the sky meets the horizon without interruption. This stop along the way near Salina shows one of the many grain filled "aircraft carriers" of the prairies.

THE LAY OF THE LAND

Few stop to think that these granite boulders in northeastern Kansas were transported by a glacier weighing billions of tons, as many as 25,000 years before our time.

Kansas land, like Kansas weather, is characterized by both the unexpected and the unusual. Although portrayed in song and story as a land of monotonous sameness—flat, dry, and empty—in reality it is a land of hills, woods, mesas, buttes, fertile plains, and virgin grasslands. A Vermonter would feel at home here in the steep, wooded hills of Leavenworth County; an Arizonan would feel comfortable in the clay-pot red soil of the mesas and buttes of Medicine Lodge country; and a sun-withered Texas ranch hand would fit well in a saddle, roaming the Flint Hills from Emporia to Wichita.

The lay of the land is, in fact, a slope, rising from east to west. Kansas is thought of as being flat; but the altitude actually varies from about 700′ above sea level in Kansas City to nearly 4000′ near the Colorado border. This tilting is gradual, however, and most travelers are not aware of the rise, caused by the erosion of the Rocky Mountains which has deposited soil on these high plains.

Kansas is a geologist's paradise. Formations created by ancient winds and waters abound throughout the state. Evidence of such natural

If you haven't been to see these limestone monoliths in Gove County, you should probably plan a trip. It is said they might be gone in another two or three million years.

artistry can be found in the chalk pillars of Gove County. Castle Rock and Monument Rocks are fossil-rich chalk pillars that rise seventy-five feet above the surface of what was once an inland sea. The artistry can be seen in the giant Mushroom Rocks in Ottawa County, where giant sandstone spheres seem to be glued to solid stems. Incongruous granite boulders—part of the glacial till to be found in northeastern Kansas—are reminders of the glacier's visit to this region. Fossil imprints track the movement of inland seas, leaving a legacy of reptile skeletons, beautifully preserved fossil seashells, and life-sustaining soil and salt, all pressed into the receptive earth. The salt reserves near Hutchinson are said to be sufficient to last the United States for over 350,000 years. These rich soils and minerals have provided the source of much of the wealth and fame enjoyed by Kansans today.

This piece of land, 411 miles long and 208 miles wide, covers over 82,000 square miles. The terrain is mainly rolling grassland, with occasional woodland along the streams and rivers. As one moves from east to west, there are fewer wooded areas and the Flint Hills begin and then join the almost uninterrupted plain. Rainfall decreases as the elevation increases. More moisture results in more vegetation in the eastern sections.

The historic geographic center of the contiguous forty-eight states of the United States is located near Lebanon, in Smith County, Kansas. In the southeast corner of Osborne County lies the geodetic center, which is used for surveys in mapping the North American continent. Kansas is, indeed, the nation's heartland!

Mushroom Rock, in Ellsworth County, south of Carneiro.

A scoop loader removes large salt chunks 645 feet below the surface at the Carey Salt Mine in Hutchinson.

This rugged section of Kansas near Medicine Lodge is not at all like the rest of the state. The canyons, outcroppings, and green spaces share the red dirt with cattle herds and pumping oil rigs.

THE KAW AND ITS COMPANIONS

High water on the Marais des Cygnes near Osawatomie.

Most of the state is drained by either the Kansas or the Arkansas river. The Arkansas begins in the mountains of Colorado and flows eastward, then south into Oklahoma. Formed by waters from the Republican, Big Blue, and Smoky Hill rivers, the Kansas begins near Junction City and flows eastward to the Missouri River, which nips off the northeastern corner of the state from Kansas City to Leavenworth and Atchison.

Most early life in the United States was tied to the rivers, and life in Kansas was no exception. Many towns such as Wichita, Manhattan, Junction City, and Kansas City developed at the confluence of rivers, mainly because of the transportation they provided.

The United States Geological Survey considers the Kansas, Republican, Smoky Hill, Arkansas, Cimarron, and Neosho rivers to be the "principal rivers of Kansas." They have served as sources of water, transportation, and power. The earliest settlers lost no time in making use of these valuable resources. Civilization centered around the early ferries and forts. The need for trade and peacekeeping caused the government to send troops to settle in what is now Kansas. In 1827 the War Department established a fort, commanded by Colonel Henry Leavenworth, who sent Moses Grinter to establish a ferry service across the Kansas River.

"... amen. David, don't reach! Ask politely and Jim can pass what you want. Where are your Sunday manners?" Dining room, Grinter House, Kansas City, Kansas.

This virgin land west of Olathe in the Prairie Center Park will never see pavement, plows, or progress. The only intruders will be people following its natural paths.

Grinter's ferry, situated south of present-day Leavenworth, became a link between the Oregon and Santa Fe trails. It was used by settlers, traders, and the army. An Indian settlement developed around the ferry. By 1833 a gristmill was turning grain into flour, and a sawmill was turning trees into lumber. The rivers thus molded the shape of life as they controlled the movement of families and supplies throughout the Midwest.

Many of these old mills, long since displaced by coal-generated power, are now tourist attractions. Among them are the Old Mill Museum in Lindsborg, which is well worth a visit, and the Oxford Mill. In Wamego, the old Dutch-style mill, transplanted stone by stone, sits prominently in the city park, where it is easier to enjoy.

Today, wildlife refuges are scattered throughout the state. The sounds of eagles and geese fill the air as the migrating flocks look for places to stop off on their flights. In summer, the eagles have to relinquish the skies above Wilson Reservoir to hang gliders. Sailboats add brilliant color and the sounds

A sudden spring shower at the Wamego Mill sends visiting school children running back to their bus.

of their sails to the summer breezes as Kansans enjoy their leisure time on the lakes and lakeshores. Twenty-one reservoirs now exist, and more are planned in connection with flood-control and mine-reclamation projects.

It was not always so. For the early homesteader, reservoirs would have been only a dream. Their search for a site with a source of water to fill farming, livestock, and family needs was sometimes very difficult. In eastern Kansas there were streams, and if a stream was not close by, a shallow well could be dug. Central and western Kansas had much less water, so the search there became one for a deep underground spring. At Greensburg in south-central Kansas, the world's largest hand-dug well, 109' deep, was completed in 1885. Although the prairies had fertile soil and rich grasses for the cattle, they were useless for the rancher-farmer unless there was a water source. This led to the introduction of the windmill, which pulled the evasive moisture to the surface so that the cattle could drink, thus making cattle ranching a possibility.

The Oxford Mill, built in 1874, still stands on the Arkansas River.

Kansas sportsmen have championed conservation for decades. Private lakes and government reservoirs have popped up in the last half-century... deer have reappeared in "herd" quantities... and flocks of wild fowl fill the air each spring.

"This may be the last nice weekend we'll have to look for bittersweet. It feels like winter."

This search for water has been a continuing thread in the story of Kansas. In recent years, irrigation has played an increasingly important role. Airplane passengers flying over Kansas are provided with a surprising view of modern farming methods. Those who are not familiar with the irrigation system wonder at the symmetrical scene below them as they cross the state. Each green circle that is visible from the air represents three-fourths of a 640-acre section using center-pivot pump irrigation. The hydraulically-propelled "walking water fountains" leave these circular patterns as they move across the fields. The more conventional water-filled ditches provide gravity-siphoned life to the fields in many areas where there is still a checkerboard pattern of kelly green wheat rather than circles.

Winter wheat near Louisburg.

THE FIRST KANSANS

As long as five thousand years before Coronado came in search of the fabled cities of gold, Indian tribes blended with nature on the land. In 1541, when Coronado and his men journeyed into Kansas and became the first white men to view these prairies, the Spaniards unknowingly left a legacy destined to change the Indian culture. Horses that wandered away from the Spanish camps became an extension of the Indian, greatly increasing both his mobility and his range. Numerous tribes lived in Kansas and left their mark on the land. The Kansa (also called Kaw, Konza, Kanza) Indians, "the people of the South Wind," gave their name to the region. Other Indian tribal names, such as Osage, Wichita, Wyandotte, and Pawnee, dot the Kansas map.

The Kansa tribe lived in northeastern Kansas; the Osage in the southeastern section of the state; the Pawnee, in the Republican River valley; and the Wichita, along the Arkansas River in central Kansas. Ruins of a pueblo settlement in Scott County show that Taos Pueblo Indians once lived there. Many nomadic Plains tribes came into the region to hunt buffalo.

The conflict between the Indians and the white man had a definite impact on the development of Kansas. The military forts, created as guardians of western growth, dotted the landscape and provided some of the first white population to the state. Travelers on the Santa Fe Trail depended on these havens of safety as they traveled across the plains. Fort Larned suffered repeated Indian attacks because of its location near Pawnee Rock, one of the most vulnerable spots on the trail. This rich Indian hunting ground, located between Great Bend and Larned, was the scene of many raids and deaths. Consequently, travelers often waited for others to come along, so as to increase their numbers before continuing, and it was not unusual

This cross, commemorating Coronado's passage through southwestern Kansas, is near Fort Dodge.

for a train of several hundred wagons to leave the fort at one time on the road to Santa Fe. Today the highway at the base of Pawnee Rock covers the ruts of the old trail. Other forts joined Fort Larned across the territory, protecting early settlers and wagon trains as they crossed the region. Many of the historic forts were abandoned soon after the Civil War because seasoned army troops, led by men like General George Custer, and scouts like Wild Bill Hickok and William F. Cody were able to defeat the Indians. The forts were ultimately sold to be made into farms or were ceded to the state. Fort Hays with 7,500 acres was given for use as a college, an agricultural experimental station, and a park. Today, only Fort Riley and Fort Leavenworth are still active. Others, such as Fort Larned,

There are three kinds of animals mentioned in "Home On the Range." Buffalo is one, can you name the other two?

The northeastern border of the state is defined by the Missouri River. This cannon at Fort Leavenworth still stands sentinel as the army base continues to play a vital role in today's military education. The pre-Civil War house still stands northwest of Leavenworth as a proud survivor.

Shawnee Methodist Mission in Fairway, on the Santa Fe and Oregon Trails, was begun by Rev. Thomas Johnson as a school for Indian children of many tribes.

Charles Curtis, vice-president of the United States under Herbert Hoover from 1928 to 1932, was the grandson of a Kansa Indian woman, whose husband, Louis Pappan, had started the ferry at Topeka. Curtis stayed in Topeka with his father's family rather than going with the tribe to Oklahoma.

Many other Indians have added a page to the history of Kansas. When Fort Scott, and Fort Hays, remain as preserved or reconstructed landmarks and have become major tourist attractions.

The Indians left Kansas in increasing numbers as the buffalo hunters depleted the great herds that these nomadic peoples had depended upon for survival. Because of the loss of their food supply and the overwhelming numbers of settlers and soldiers, the Indians finally gave up the fight and moved to government-supplied land in Oklahoma by the 1870's.

The early Chase County bridge builders may have been inspired by the Roman aqueducts.

Baptiste Peoria, chief of the Peoria, was forced to emigrate with his tribe to Kansas from Illinois, he settled in Miami County in what is now Paola. Some say that members of his tribe pronounced his name "Paolay" and that the town was named for him. Peoria Street in Paola was definitely named for him and the first post office was called Peoria Village. Baptiste and his wife were most anxious for Paola to grow and prosper. They gave the land for a church and for a park square to be used for play and recreation. Legend says that the Indians raced their ponies there in the town's early days. Baptiste later moved his tribe to Oklahoma.

Only a few tribes remained by the early 1870's—the Sac, the Fox, the Kickapoo, the Potawatomi, and a few Miami. Council Grove, Medicine Lodge, the Shawnee Methodist Indian Mission in Fairway, the Wyandotte Methodist Mission, the Osage Mission in Neosho County, the Catholic Mission at St. Mary's, the Potawatomi Baptist Mission in Topeka, and the Ottawa Baptist Mission all have their place in Kansas history books as the sites where Indian treaties were made or where religious institutions were set up to help educate the Indians to the way of life of the white man. These are now preserved as museums and monuments to the heritage of these great Indian cultures, which lived as one with the land that was to become Kansas.

The history of Fort Scott, one of the first military establishments in the southeastern part of the state, lives on at this reconstructed site.

Overleaf: *This fine old stone ranch house and barn, built of native post rock limestone, sits in the Republican river valley south of Scandia.*

The strawberries are gone from Strawberry Hill in Kansas City, but the rich ethnic blend of cultures remains.

MANY BACKGROUNDS

Kansas was molded by contacts with many cultures. Before becoming a part of the United States, the area was claimed by Spain, England, France, Mexico, and the Republic of Texas. Explorers, traveling through the land, reported on the flora, fauna, and Indian tribes that they saw on their journeys. Meriwether Lewis and William Clark crossed the area in 1804, Zebulon Pike explored it in 1806, and Major Stephen Long came in 1819. It was Long's map that labeled the region "the Great American Desert." John C. Fremont, who camped in the hills of Wabaunsee County in 1842 while on a surveying trip, reported back that the area of Kansas had great agricultural potential. However, because of the frequently expressed idea that the area was uninhabitable, the desert myth prevailed, and the territory was left to the Indian tribes.

From the opening of the Kansas-Nebraska territory to white settlement in 1854 until the outbreak of the Civil War in 1861, the territory of Kansas was the center of political and social tumult. Earlier inhabitants had been limited to Indian tribes, soldiers in scattered forts, Indian missionaries, and those other brave souls who ventured into Indian territory. From 1854 to 1861 Northern and Southern sympathizers used their strength and resources to send settlers to the territory. Members of each side were convinced that the slavery question could be settled by having Kansas enter the Union on "their" side. The tragedy of the Civil War can be said to have really begun in "Bleeding Kansas," where the two sides confronted each other. Beecher Bible and Rifle Church in Wabaunsee is an example of the extent of the emotion involved. "Beecher's Bibles" were rifles, named for Henry Ward Beecher, who felt that the evils of slavery justified the use of violence. He was the brother of Harriet Beecher Stowe, the author of *Uncle Tom's Cabin,* described by Abraham Lincoln as the "little woman who started the big war." Beecher, a Congregational minister in Brooklyn, New York, thought that a better method of stopping the spread of slavery would be to equip Free State emigrants with Sharp's rifles and Colt Navy revolvers, the latest advancement in firearms, rather than Bibles and prayer books. John Brown was another militant abolitionist whose attempts to end slavery included a great deal of violent activity around Osawatomie. Lawrence, Topeka, and Manhattan were centers of antislavery sentiment; Leavenworth and Atchison were founded by Missourians who hoped to move great numbers of proslavery voters into Kansas. The Civil War interrupted development in the territory which had achieved statehood on the 29th of January in 1861, for the war that was raging in the East severely affected the lives of most Kansans. "Bleeding Kansas" had suffered turmoil as abolitionists and proslavery factions were confronting one another. When war was officially declared, many Kansans signed up.

The pandemonium over the slavery question exploded again in Kansas with Quantrill's Raid on Lawrence in 1863, which caused more than 150 deaths. The Battle of Westport, Missouri, in 1864, spilled over into Kansas as the Confederates retreated. The Battle of Mine Creek in Linn County was decisive in the defeat of the Confederates.

After the Civil War, the Homestead Act opened the area to those who desired to leave the East and to search for a new and better future on the frontier. Hardy, determined homesteaders came to find new lives. They established communities, built homes with whatever could be found, planted crops, had families, and became a part of the Kansas heritage. John Greenleaf Whittier, in "The Kansas Emigrant," described their travels:

"We cross the prairies as of old
    The Pilgrims crossed the sea,
To make the West, as they the East,
    The homestead of the free."

The hard work and persistence of the homesteaders during the lonely days, often under dismal conditions, helped to develop the strength that has been honored by later generations. Living in rude dwellings, they faced bare, treeless, sun-parched plains. Their astonishing bravery was evidenced in their confrontations with wild animals; prairie fires; accidents which were faced with little or no medical help; and natural calamities. Blizzards, floods, tornadoes, locust plagues, and droughts were all faced and conquered by the homesteaders.

The ingenuity of many settlers was tested immediately upon arrival as they set about the task of building a home. Those in eastern and central Kansas had wood and stone to use. Those in western Kansas, however, found that there were not enough trees to use for building, nor was workable rock or stone available. The sod house was the ideal answer to their problem, so earthen dwellings were the homesteaders' early homes. Dugouts, incorporating many principles of today's earth-sheltered houses, provided many with their first protection, albeit damp, dark, and insect-ridden. Sod houses, fashioned of blocks of sod, cut and piled like bricks, were built to replace the dugouts. As time passed, these were often modernized by adding shingled roofs, frame windows, or frame

A meadowlark sings its spirited song from atop a corner post with its rock cairn support.

additions to the original house. As money and trade made wood more readily available, the "soddies" were often abandoned. Most of them survive only in pictures, in museum displays, or in the memories of those who were fortunate enough to encounter a soddy as a child.

The limestone in central Kansas was easily quarried and was used in creating houses, barns, bridges, churches, schools, courthouses and other public buildings. Uses for the stone seemed almost endless to the early settlers, and they honed their skills of masonry in making the intricate patterns which they laid with great care. Their barns and houses store untold tales. Perhaps the most innovative use of the stone was for making fenceposts, thousands of which are still to be seen today, serving their original purpose. Post-rock country is famous throughout the nation. Museums document how men struggled to break the 250 to 500-pound posts loose from the limestone ledges; their wedges, hammers, and other tools and supplies are exhibited. The visitor can even purchase a miniature stone fencepost, accompanied by details such as: "40,000 miles of fence built in fifty years using stone posts"; "Barbed wire was plentiful, but timber scarce."

People came to Kansas from all parts of the nation and the world. The majority came from the East Coast and from Illinois, Ohio, Indiana, and Missouri. About fifty

School children in Nicodemus jump on the "runaway stage," make a giant leap to catch the "riverboat" as it pulls away from the dock, and sprint to catch the "last train" as it leaves the station.

the life style that they had developed in Germany and Russia. The Turkey Red winter wheat they carried with them has developed into the crop that is still synonymous with the word Kansas today.

Swedish immigrants arrived after a severe drought in Sweden; their ancestors are still found throughout the state. Lindsborg is a center for Swedish heritage, and bits of Sweden are evident throughout the city. English settlers also arrived, but they were not as successful in

Bethany Place, a former girls' school near the state capitol in Topeka, now serves as the headquarters for the Episcopal Diocese of Kansas.

thousand blacks came to Kansas after the Civil War. Nicodemus was formed by many former slaves who came to begin their lives of freedom there.

Immigrants from abroad also added to the Kansas population. Germany provided the German-Russian Mennonites who came to Marion, McPherson, Harvey, and Reno counties, bringing with them

There were four things every general store needed ... white paint, a front porch roof, a Coca Cola sign on the side and Rainbo stenciled on the front screens. This store in Industry has them all.

adapting to the new life. Many were wealthy and tried to follow the customs of their family and friends in Britain. Few succeeded, though they did leave their mark. Mexican immigrants came to work on the railroad or on sugar beet farms. Italians settled in the eastern part of the state in the mining areas of Crawford County. Other ethnic groups joined these settlers in helping Kansas to become a melting pot of nationalities. Many festivals are held annually throughout the state to celebrate the role of different ethnic groups in the creation of Kansas.

What's in a name? Viewing a map of Kansas, one can see the unbridled optimism of those early settlers reflected in such names as Independence, Enterprise, Industry, Home, Eureka, Paradise, and Protection. Other place names gave honor to earlier homes: Scandia, Hanover, New Albany, New Lancaster. Some settlers viewed their surroundings and took a key from them: Burr Oak, Lone Elm, Sylvan Grove, Oak Hill, Sycamore Woods—all show the value of the trees and the glory of the land on which the towns were located. Physical features abound in place names: Great Bend, Hill City, Junction City, Prairie Village, Valley Center, Pretty Prairie, Plains, Mound City. Natural resources also played a role in the selection process: Galena, Gas City, Mineral, Gem, Gypsum. Indian names appear frequently, referring to the beauty and the glory of the land. Names of Spanish, French, English, German, Greek, and Latin origin are also found.

Other names honor important early settlers, or perhaps an incident would give a town its identity. It is said that Liberal received its name from the generous nature of S. S. Rogers, who homesteaded in the southwestern Kansas area in 1872 and dug a deep well. Water was scarce in that section of the state, but travelers could always depend on him for a cool drink and could receive all the water they wanted. When told that the water was free, they often would reply, "That's liberal, friend, mighty liberal."

To these deeply devoted people, religion provided the source of their courage and faith. It is no

Even people who have never been to Cottonwood Falls in Chase County can take one look at this scene and feel what is meant by city squares, county seats, and old court houses.

surprise, then, that Saints Peter, Paul, Francis, Mary, George, and John appear on the Kansas map.

Kansas still has a legacy dedicated to this strong faith. Church spires punctuate the Kansas landscape. Handhewn limestone structures, which dominate the landscape in many towns such as Victoria, are a memorial to their devotion and dedication. The twin spires of St. Fidelis Church in Victoria tower 140 feet, reaching for the heavens. Religious immigrants from Germany and Russia helped to build this "Cathedral of the Plains" by donating loads of stone and giving money to show their devotion to God and to their new homeland. St. Joseph's Church in Damar stands on the Kansas plains "as a sentinel guarding its flock." It, too, was built by its congregation.

Devotion to their faith and to their land has played an important part in the life of Kansans. The character of the people seems to reflect this closeness to religion and to the soil—even in those whose lives are far removed from farming. The spirit of Kansas is filled with a sense of humanity, with compassion, and with a love for this land. John J. Ingalls, who served Kansas as a United States senator for eighteen years, was an idealist whose loyalty to the state was inspirational. A quote reflects his feeling for the state: "He affirmed that once a man had become a citizen of Kansas, his allegiance to the State could never be alienated or forsworn. So potent is the spell with which Kansas binds her children, that they might wander, might roam, might live in other lands, but could never be other than Kansans."

Carl Becker, a highly respected historian, wrote a 1910 essay titled "Kansas" that is filled with respect for the Kansas spirit. In it he describes listening to two college girls on a train to Lawrence. Their chatter was interrupted as they looked out the window and saw the cornfields and sunflowers growing by the side of the railroad track. One said, "Dear Old Kansas!" Becker states, "To understand why people say 'Dear Old Kansas!' is to understand that Kansas is no mere geographical expression, but a 'state of mind,' a religion, and a philosophy in one." Kansas is "accumulated traditions, religious creeds, political institutions, and intellectual conceptions." "The result has been to give a peculiar flavor to the Kansas spirit of individualism. With Kansas history back of him, the true Kansan feels that nothing is *too much* for him."

Living a modest, frugal, deeply religious life, the Amish provide a contrast, yet harmonize with their south central Kansas neighbors.

Many of the finest churches in Kansas are in the remotest locations. St. Joseph's Church in Damar pops out of the fields with twin spires visible for miles around.

WELL WORN PATHS

Before settlement began in earnest, the area which is now Kansas was a quiet wilderness, almost undisturbed. Blizzards, droughts, dust storms, floods, tornadoes, and prairie fires were experienced only by the Indian tribes who lived in the area, and by the grasshoppers, coyotes, and the buffalo. During the one hundred years after the Kansas-Nebraska Act was passed, the wilderness changed unbelievably. It was penetrated by trail blazers, Indian fighters, wagon trains, stagecoaches, railroads, cattle drives, and Conestoga wagons filled with homesteaders headed for new lives and incredible adventure.

Glowing reports of easily gained riches helped to attract many through the region with the establishment of the Santa Fe and Oregon trails. William Becknell traced the trail to Santa Fe, and countless others followed this trade route in search of quick profits. The California Gold Rush also drew fortune hunters through the area. As more and more Americans passed through the land, soldiers came to protect them. Forts gave birth to towns. Some travel-weary souls elected to stay rather than to continue their travel west, thus peopling the plains which had for so long been thought useless.

The Santa Fe Trail left Westport, Missouri, and crossed over into Kansas in present-day Johnson County, angled southwest through Council Grove toward Pawnee Rock, then along the banks of the Arkansas River, across the Cimarron and on into Santa Fe, where trade with the Spanish flourished. About two-thirds of the trail was in Kansas. Another major route, the Oregon-California Trail, passed through northeastern Kansas, then proceeded north into Nebraska and west along the Platte River to California or Oregon. Some who started the journey would become disillusioned and return to Kansas to live. In "Comin' Back to Kansas," a song collected from Mrs. Clara Ballard in Butler County, Kansas, this phenomenon is recorded:

"They are comin' back to Kansas,
 They are crossin' on the bridge,
 You can see their mover wagons,
 On the top of every ridge,

On the highways and the turnpikes,
You can see their wagons come,
For they're comin' back to Kansas,
And they're comin' on the run."

Half of America will never get the opportunity to view a scene like this. The enormity of the clouds almost overpowers the peeking sun and pastoral countryside.

The wagons have become a part of our folklore. The prairie schooner is a familiar sight to today's youngsters who watch movies and TV shows. The wagon wheel ruts that remain today, dug so deeply into the Kansas soil by the countless wayfarers, can still be seen from the air in many places. One such spot is outside of Gardner, where the Oregon and Santa Fe trails split.

Settlers and wagon trains were followed by a different sort of traffic, making trails, not of wagon ruts, but of cattle hooves. Although movies and TV shows have romanticized the period of the cattle drives into a drama that seems to encompass a good part of a century, the period of the cattle drives was actually rather short. The cross-country cattle trade from Texas to Kansas began in the 1860's and ended in the 1880's. The drives began when Texas cattle were herded to Kansas for shipment by rail to eastern markets, where the demand was great, supplies having dwindled during the Civil War. Railroad boom towns—Abilene, Ellsworth, Newton, Wichita, and Dodge City—swelled in population and wealth as the cattle were shipped through their railheads. The Chisholm Trail became a household word, even in the East, and any trail from Texas to a Kansas railhead was given that name.

The official Kansas state song, "Home on the Range," was written in the 1870's. It reflects some of this romance with the cowboy out under the stars in the pure Kansas air— "Where seldom is heard a discouraging word / And the sky is not clouded all day."

The cattle drives ended for many reasons. The railroad reached Texas; cattle prices fell; Kansas homesteaders fenced in more and more land with barbed wire, blocking the trails; communities developed; and the Kansas cattle breeders began to fear that the diseases being brought in by the herds of Texas cattle might infect their own improving herds. George Grant of Victoria, Kansas, imported the first Aberdeen-Angus cattle to America in 1873 from Scotland. They were crossed with native longhorns. In 1885 the Kansas Legislature finally passed a law to exclude the Texas herds, thus closing the door on a brief but colorful chapter of Kansas history. The period provided us with many legends and created heroes to be emulated by young cowboys to this day. Stories of Wild Bill Hickok, Bat Masterson, Wyatt Earp, the Dalton Gang, and other lawmen and badmen have filled the screens. TV, movies, and recreated cow towns, such as those in Dodge City and Wichita, help to keep the dream alive. All this would no doubt bring a chuckle to those who actually lived in the mud, dust, and killing winters of those infant communities.

Although the cowboy boom days were short-lived, the railway made possible the shipment of larger numbers of southwestern cattle to fatten on the bluestem grasses of the Flint Hills.

The role of the railroads in settling Kansas was vital. Early explorers had written uninviting accounts of the territory. The "Great American Desert" reputation was strong. As an incentive to get the railroads into the West, the federal government gave them ten million acres of land adjoining their tracks. The enthusiastic railroads often overglamorized their sales pitches

This landmark stands at the end of Front Street as a reminder of the cattle drives that put Dodge City on the map.

The old west tradition is alive even today in this western Kansas mail box.

for the new territory to lure settlers to the area. The Kansas Pacific Railroad, created in the early 1860's, had crossed the state and reached Denver by 1870. This branch of the Union Pacific was to bring many homesteaders into the new state.

Cyrus K. Holliday was the father of the Santa Fe railroad. He prepared the charter for the Atchison and Topeka railroad and sold others on his dream of a railroad line that would extend to the city of Santa Fe. In 1868 he predicted that the line would reach the Pacific Ocean and the Gulf of Mexico, but was considered a lunatic. Years later he was considered a prophet! The Atchison and Topeka railroad was begun in October of 1868 with the first spadeful of dirt dug in Topeka. It reached Newton's cattle pens in

Overleaf: *This Kansas windmill stands as a single sentinel against the oncoming storm.*

Although the Pony Express only lasted eighteen months in Kansas, the Hollenberg Station, near Hanover, has survived for over 100 years in unaltered condition.

Once a common sight around railroad depots, these baggage carts have gone the way of steam locomotives and wooden water towers.

"All aboard. Last train leaving Cherryvale."

Flashing red lights speak the language of the rails.

1871 and extended to the Kansas-Colorado border in early 1873. Few towns existed west of Emporia before the coming of the train, but railroad officials drew up plats and named new towns to be populated later.

The railroads' sales pitches, along with those of land speculators and town-site promoters, helped to bring many people to Kansas during the period after the Civil War. The railroads even sent out brochures praising the advantages that Kansas had to offer as both haven and hope for immigrants. These brochures reached not only the towns of the East but Europe as well. Many settlers arrived to fulfill their American dream, but found the communities only in the planning stages. These determined optimists rolled up their sleeves and stayed to build Kansas towns and cities.

Not much remains of Holliday, a once important railroad town on the Kaw River southwest of Kansas City, but C. K. Holliday's vision grew into the mighty Atchison, Topeka and Santa Fe.

Long before Sputnik, shuttles, and Star Wars, the monsters of the plains roared and steamed through the fields. Now they roar and steam only at threshing demonstrations like this one at the Agricultural Hall of Fame near Bonner Springs.

GIFTS FROM THE LAND

Kansas was born as a land of Indians and buffalo, but it has grown to become an agricultural giant, providing approximately one-fifth of the wheat produced in the United States, more than any comparable area of the country. Many early settlers were farmers. Prior to the arrival of Turkey Red, the hard winter wheat that was brought by the Mennonites, corn was the principal crop, and it continues to be important today. The shift from grassland to grain crops produced the farm scene of today, in which wheat predominates.

In areas that are unsuited to grain, cattle play a major role. Kansas is third in beef production in the nation. Much of the plains region of Kansas is covered by limestone ridges sprinkled with flint (3.7 million acres in the Flint Hills). This land is not suitable for cultivation, but is very appropriate for grazing cattle. Its plateaus and ravines are covered with prairie grasses, and a visitor can see the cattle working their way across in search of water and a more appetizing morsel of grass. The Cimarron National Grassland, in the southwest corner of Kansas near Elkhart, is also good cattle country.

The Konza Prairie Research Natural Area near Fort Riley and Manhattan covers 8,616 acres of Flint Hills that are being preserved for ecological research and education. The scrubby cedars and coarse stems of native bluestem grasses can be seen on the dry ravines and rolling hillsides, as yet

"Well, what do you think? Do we take it?"
"Looks pretty good to me."

undisturbed by the plow. Research is done here to study the natural prairie ecosystem in order to compare it with the cultivated and grazed prairie. It is not a public-use area, and visits are not encouraged because research projects are being conducted on site by faculty, students, and scientists from Kansas State University and other institutions. Persons walking through the prairie might disturb conditions in a way that would invalidate the research. One can view the area from surrounding roads and imagine early Kansas, with its virgin prairie intact. Some native animals have been reintroduced to the natural

Counting trucks lined up at the elevator at harvest time is like counting cars on a passing freight.

"Who'd have thought with all of the rain, the late freeze, and the bugs that we'd get a record yield." You can almost feel the June heat on this harvest day near Abilene.

ecosystem so that conditions can be much the same as they were originally.

As settlers began to put their stamp upon the land, the plains took on a new look. No longer did the vast and seemingly unending grasses, which fed the buffalo herds, fill the horizon throughout the state. Instead, swaying oceans of grain, golden in the sunlight, greeted the onlookers as they passed by.

Russian settlers had brought many things with them from the old country: values, traditions, and ideas, but most important, the seed grain for a hard winter wheat. Settling near Newton, these German-Russian Mennonites planted Turkey Red, the variety of winter wheat that grew under similar conditions in Russia. These early farmers could never have predicted that this hardy wheat would be developed into a grain which would become a world leader. This miracle of plenty, which

It's on days like this, after the cattle have been fed, that the Flint Hills ranchers can sit back, talk about next year... and let nature work below the snow.

Scientists visit their research project at the Konza Prairie Natural Area.

Only a Kansan would consider an annual burn-off of the prairie. For as long as many can remember, the Flint Hills have been burned each spring to help the new grass grow. Not everyone agrees with this practice. Sometimes a bolt of lightning stops all arguments.

is produced every year in Kansas, makes agriculture a multimillion-dollar industry for the state. Although wheat is the major Kansas crop, sorghum, corn, hay, and other crops are significant.

Grain elevators, similar to those shown earlier, are a common sight,

In contrast to its carefully pruned cousins in Doniphan County's orchards, this apple tree near Springhill drops its apples untended.

towering like urban skyscrapers over the Kansas landscape. Hutchinson's half-mile-long silos, which hold 17 million bushels, are duplicated in smaller versions across the state, all holding the yearly harvest of grains. At harvest

"What says springtime better than apple blossoms?"

49

"You're right, that was the noon whistle and he's late with our lunch."

No barnyard is complete without its mother cat and kittens.

time the silos are near to bursting with the gifts of the fields. In an especially abundant harvest, grain can be seen piled high in the center of a town or around the already filled silos.

Wheat fields, with the winds rippling through the oceans of ripening grain awaiting the harvest, provide a beautiful picture of summer in Kansas. The convoys of harvesting equipment and crews

It is obvious that the New England influence was present when the owner of this unique three level barn designed the structure to fit the terrain south of Beaumont.

One day "Oreo" may be a county fair winner.
There'll be lots of personal care till then.

This is what is meant by range-fed beef . . .
enjoying the green grass and rain-filled pond
in early summer before nature and the heat
paint everything brown.

Late afternoon sun catches the roof top and highlights the traces of early snow.

A surviving rarity in southeast Kansas on 69 highway near Fort Scott.

Elevator, near Russell

converge on Kansas in July, ready to reap the bountiful fields. Soon, men and women working in the fields, dripping with perspiration and exhausted by heat and dust, will deliver truckloads of ripened grain to these elevators, to be sent from there on train and ship to help feed the people of our country and foreign countries as well.

"Oceans of grain" is an apt metaphor. To bend over, gleaning a few stalks of wheat left behind by the combine in the corner of a field and being brushed by the steady blowing breeze of early evening, can produce the same dizzy seasick feeling as can rolling ocean waves. Standing in the fields, listening to the sounds of the whistling wheat, the romance and lure of farming could be easily understood. Have you ever stood in a cornfield on a hot summer night and listened? There are those who say you can actually hear the growing process. The whistling of the wheat gives a similar feeling: you become a part of nature and the process of life, itself.

Feeling the scorching wind blowing against their faces as the early farmers must have felt it, today's farmers must feel that the air-conditioned combines that can glean entire fields in one afternoon are indeed modern miracle machines. Building on the heritage of early hard-working settlers, Kansas has fulfilled the prediction of many and has become an important contributor to the breadbasket of the world.

Nothing quite says October like this fruit stand near Edwardsville.

When the Sunflowers Bloom

(Albert Bigelow Paine)

"I've been off on a journey; I jes' got home to-day;
I traveled east, an' north, an' south, an' every other way;
I seen a heap of country, an' cities on the boom,
But I want to be in Kansas when the
    Sun-
        Flowers
            Bloom."

"When all the sky above is jest ez blue ez blue kin be,
an' the prairies air a wavin' like a yaller driftin' sea,
Oh, it's there my soul goes sailin' an' my heart is on the boom
In the golden fields of Kansas when the
    Sun-
        Flowers
            Bloom."

Dry grasses welcome the coming storm.

Things are not always what they seem. These barns in Johnson and Wyandotte Counties both give every appearance of containing hay bales, livestock stalls, and farm machinery. Unlike the Johnson County barn, milking chores, hay storage, or the raising of championship livestock will never be a part of the activity in the barn on page fifty-nine. This barn, located adjacent to the Missouri River in Wyandotte County, is part of the presedimentation facilities for Water District No. 1 of Johnson County. It houses a different type of machinery, the chemical feed, pumping station, and control center, and also contains a laboratory and offices.

When purchasing the land, representatives of Black and Veatch were challenged by the property owner to build a station which would not disturb his rustic view, but blend into the rural scenery around it. The challenge was met with the shingle-roofed, cedar-sided barn. Unlike the typical barn, this will never face the destructive decay of wood rot on its foundation and support structure. It won't begin to tilt and lean, and then fall as its timbers crumble.

Johnson County barn.

Time and weather cannot so easily demolish the interior concrete and steel, so the structure will silhouette the horizon and help to provide drinking water for years to come.

This barn, located adjacent to the Missouri River in Wyandotte County, is part of the presedimentation facilities for Water District No. 1 of Johnson County.

Don't let any pig tell you this is fun. Sometimes it takes a boot in the ham hock to get porky in the special bath.

Nothing says open road more than I-70 near Goodland.

INDUSTRY THRIVES

Although agribusiness is the primary industry of Kansas today and other industries related to the earth's bounty dominate the state's economy, they are by no means the only ones.

Industry developed in Kansas, as it had elsewhere, around the available raw materials and in response to the needs of the people. The earliest industries in the state were related to transportation. First, the goods that were needed to outfit and supply those setting out on the trails were provided. Wagons were built and sold, and trading posts sprang up to meet the demand. Then the railroad industry followed. Hundreds were employed to lay the

Wooden towers once dotted the landscape in coal mining areas of southeastern Kansas. More modern methods made them obsolete.

rails for the iron horse, and the resulting rapid transportation allowed new businesses to develop and prosper. As communities grew, sawmills, grain mills, and other businesses that were allied to the booming growth expanded rapidly. Many truck lines whose familiar markings are seen well beyond Kansas borders have their home offices in Kansas today.

Businesses using the abundant Kansas raw materials provided plentiful opportunities for work. Coal mines, salt mines; the oil, natural gas, and helium industries – all employed large numbers in exploration, development, and distribution. Even today these industries continue to flourish. Other minerals were also put to work by astute businessmen. Soon, clay bricks were being shipped throughout the area. Museums display mementos of this thriving trade. Coffeyville, Diamond, Columbus, Fredonia, Fort Scott, Humboldt, Iola, Lawrence, Pittsburg, Topeka, Neodesha, Chanute, Atchison, and many other city names grace the surfaces of bricks that have survived the ravages

An early predecessor of the farm implements made in Hesston today, this basket windmill in Hillsboro adjoins the Mennonite Museum.

of time and wear. Several cities paved their streets with two layers of brick, so that, when these streets were "modernized" and replaced, the pattern on the bottom layer of bricks had not been worn away. These are prized by collectors of pavers. Many of our brick streets and highways were simply covered over with more modern material to await discovery by future Kansans who may uncover them generations from now. Tales have grown up about actual characters and early experiences in Kansas industrial development. A fascinating one is about the renowned Indian Joe and his lightning speed and skill in laying paver bricks: Joe kept three men busy just supplying him as he labored. There is also a theory about the reasons for the existence of so many different brands of Kansas brick. When the federal government funded the building of roads, the states were responsible for getting the work completed. County commissioners felt strongly that the bricks for their section of the road should come from a brickyard in their own county; so when the road-building teams reached a county seat, they had to switch to bricks made in the local county.

As it is sometimes possible to discover much about a city or a state's history by reading street names, so, too, can the history of Kansas brickyards be found in the bricks that remain. Sunflowers blossom on the clay-red Columbus bricks, while an oxen yoke embellishes those from the Yoke Vitrified Brick Company of Coffeyville. Dr. Samuel J. Crumbine, secretary of the State Board of Health during the early 1900s, was responsible for another brick, popular among collectors. Because of the spread of tuberculosis, his concern for health and sanitation generated the now-famous slogan which appeared on bricks around 1908: "Don't Spit on Sidewalk." The selling price for one of these bricks is around $25.00 today!

Petroleum, helium, and natural gas production result in economic opportunities extending throughout Kansas. Chanute's oil field equipment and supply plants and natural gas wells and oil refineries near El Dorado join countless other businesses capitalizing on these natural resources. The Hugoton Gas field, one of the world's largest natural gas deposits, and the Mid-Continent Oil field, the country's largest, are famous nation-wide.

Indian legends tell of councils held around burning springs and of cures provided by the oily waters. Pioneers used the heavy oil for medicine and to grease their wagon wheels. The first successful commercial oil well west of the Mississippi was Norman No. 1, drilled in 1892 near Neodesha. Oil derricks and pumpers are common sights in Kansas today.

Left: McCoy #1 is mirrored in its pond near Garden City.

Scenes like this one, which highlights jet engine nacelle work, are commonplace at Boeing's 865-acre facility in Wichita.

This St. Mary's scene tells many stories. An early crossing of the Kaw was near here; the rich bottom land still produces bumper crops; and, in the distance, one of the country's most modern power plants helps fuel new industry, homes, and schools.

The "Mighty Sampson" over the Cimarron River is one of the largest bridges of its kind. Shifting quicksand necessitated support pylons to a depth of 165 feet. Helium storage domes are visible behind the bridge.

As roads and highways changed from brick to macadam and concrete, cement plants appeared that crushed limestone into powder and processed it to provide raw material for houses, office buildings, roads, and countless other uses across the nation. Lead and zinc, found in southeastern Kansas, were mined for use in other industrial processes.

In the 1920's the aircraft business began in Wichita. Cessna, Beech, Lear, and Boeing have helped to make that city the "air capital of the world." Attention was focused on a Kansan in 1932 when Amelia Earhart became the first woman to fly solo across the Atlantic Ocean. The production of a portion of the Saturn V space rockets by Boeing, the largest employer in the state, helped to propel Kansas into the space age, as did Kansas Astronaut Ron Evans in 1972, when he served as commander during the flight of Apollo 17 to the moon, and astronaut Joe Engle, another Kansan, when he piloted the spacecraft Columbia in November 1981. The University of Kansas flag and Jayhawk that Engle carried with him on the flight are on display at the Adams Alumni Center in Lawrence.

Many other businesses have developed and prospered in the state. Aviation guidance and communication systems are produced by King Radio Corporation in Olathe. Farm machinery is a natural. Allis-Chalmers in Topeka and Hesston Corporation in Hesston are good examples. Goodyear Tire and Rubber Company in Topeka, the auto industry in Kansas City, food processing plants in many Kansas cities, printing companies in Lawrence and elsewhere, Dupont and Coleman in Wichita, and Westinghouse in Salina are but a few of the many.

Industrial growth continues in Kansas. Research by the Kansas Department of Economic Development indicates that in an eleven-year period over fifteen hundred new firms created jobs and invested $2 billion, while existing firms expanded and provided $2.7 billion in investment.

From soil to suburbs, Kansas has definitely lived up to its motto: "Ad Astra per Aspera"—to the stars through difficulties.

The delicate lines of the hay rake are silhouetted against an early evening sky. Replaced by more efficient farm machinery, many of these rusting implements are now appreciated for their simple beauty.

All Kansas is reading, thinking, doing; seeing, hoping, testing; believing, trying, accomplishing. Everywhere within the state a great page in the history of Kansas progress is being written by ambitious, forward-looking Kansans.
—*Governor Arthur Capper*

KANSAS CULTURE

Education is a vital function of life in Kansas. It is an industry that employs thousands. State universities, private colleges and universities are joined by an extensive system of junior colleges in the state along with public community colleges, private two-year colleges, and a federal Indian junior college—Haskell at Lawrence—to provide higher education. Haskell, which opened in 1884, is among the oldest educational institutions to be given support by the United States government.

"The lesson for tomorrow will be on John Brown, the Jayhawks, and Quantrill. Ask your parents if you need help."

Left: The setting sun casts long shadows from the many towers of Anderson Hall at Kansas State University in Manhattan.

Interior of the Senate Chamber, Capitol Building, Topeka.

Statistics from the Kansas Department of Education show that the average Kansan is better educated than the national average and that Kansas ranks among the top ten states in the percentage of population that have graduated from high school. Kansas has, per capita, more colleges than forty-seven other states. State school districts stress quality in education, and many of the thirty thousand high school students who graduate in any one year go on to higher learning. Education is also a high priority to the state legislature; more than half of all tax dollars collected in the state go for education.

Kansas government is based in Topeka, the state's capital since 1861. Kansas has a bicameral legislature. Forty senators and 125 representatives serve their constituents from their offices in the Capitol. Senators serve four-year terms; representatives, two-year

There's a reassuring sense of stability to this scene at Clay Center. The strength and tradition of this area come through loud and clear... in a quiet way.

Douglas County Court House, Lawrence.

terms. The governor of Kansas serves a four-year term. The Kansas Supreme Court is the highest state court. There are 105 counties and 625 incorporated cities in Kansas. County commissioners serve four-year terms. Most cities and towns use the mayor-council form of government although some have city managers.

Several Kansans have achieved national attention in the realm of government. Edmund G. Ross, a United States Senator from Kansas, voted against the wishes of many Republicans and is remembered for having cast the deciding vote against the conviction of President Andrew Johnson in the chaotic post-Civil War period. United States Senator John J. Ingalls is revered as an orator and as a writer whose dedication to the state was eloquently presented. It was he who suggested the motto, "Ad Astra per Aspera." Charles Curtis of Topeka was the thirty-first vice-president of the United States. Dwight D. Eisenhower, who was reared in Abilene, was the thirty-fourth president of the United States from 1953 to 1961. He is buried in the church on the grounds of the Eisenhower Center in Abilene, which contains a library, a museum, and the family home in which President Eisenhower had once lived. Alfred M. Landon, governor of Kansas from 1933 to 1937, was the Republican nominee for president in 1936. Senator Robert Dole was the Republican candidate for vice-president in 1976. The first Kansas woman to be elected to fill a full term in the United States Senate is Nancy Landon Kassebaum, daughter of Alf Landon. She was elected in 1978.

Medicine Lodge home of Carrie Nation, temperance leader.

Busloads of children break out across the grounds in Abilene much like the budding and blossoming of trees and flowers at the Eisenhower Center. Ike would probably be pleased with this on-going link to Kansas youth.

Menninger Foundation, Topeka.

The healing arts have developed along with other elements of life in Kansas. From the time of rudimentary care given by family and neighbors, to the days of modern medical complexes that are available in the cities of the twentieth century, amazing accomplishments have been made. In 1925 the Menninger Clinic in Topeka was begun by Dr. C. F. Menninger; it has been continued by his sons and grandsons. The fame of this neuropsychiatric institute has spread world-wide and

Cedar Crest has the distinction of being the largest land area in the country allocated for a governor's mansion. Topeka and Menninger Hospital have been good neighbors for years. Today the bond is even closer with the governor's mansion right next door.

Known as Bell Memorial by many old timers, this building serves as the administration building for the sprawling complex of Kansas University Medical Center in Kansas City, Kansas.

Legend has it that Buffalo Bill was a guest one night at the hotel. Today's guests are mostly in for an evening of old-fashioned hospitality and the famous fried chicken dinners!

Sun sets at the end of a perfect day of sailing.

has made Topeka the mental health center for the country. Not only is treatment carried out there, but education and research in the field revolves around the institution.

The Medical Center of the University of Kansas is located in Kansas City, Kansas. Patients travel long distances for treatment. Hundreds of doctors have earned their degrees from KU and have gone on to serve the towns and cities of the state.

The sun shines more than sixty-five percent of the year on Kansas, and innumerable opportunities are available for leisure activities. Open countryside is still plentiful within a reasonable amount of driving time, even in most large cities. Jogging, bicycling, ballooning, golfing, horseback riding, hunting, fishing, camping, and water sports are popular activities. Flood-control projects have created lakes and reservoirs, so that Kansas now has 158,000 surface acres of water which provide ample chances for sailing,

'Tis said that Dorothy returned from Oz in a vehicle much like this one. Today's explorers gather at dawn and dusk to literally see which way the wind is blowing.

swimming, and other water sports. Wildlife refuges also abound. The thrill of watching the abundant quail, pheasant, geese, and ducks is surpassed only by that of spotting the rarer sandhill and whooping cranes, white pelicans, eagles, and other birds that can be seen in the Cheyenne Bottoms or in many other stopping-off places in the Central Waterfowl Flyway. Antelope, deer, prairie dogs, buffalo, and other wild species are protected in the state's game preserves.

Rodeos, fairs, and festivals punctuate the summer calendar and provide entertainment for many. There is not actually a fair in every Kansas town, but when warm weather arrives, this almost seems to be so. Fairs and rodeos fill the days of summer throughout Kansas, and over a million people attend. The rodeos begin in early May, and the season climaxes in September, with the largest fair of them all, the Kansas State Fair in Hutchinson. Excited throngs of young and old alike crowd the fairgrounds and rodeo grandstands. At the State Fair, the smells of cotton candy, hot pretzels, hot dogs, and other

Kansas City Country Club golf course in Mission Hills.

The Louis Vieux Elm east of Wamego was the Kansas champion in 1978 and has been the United States champion elm since 1979. Members of the Kansas Arborist Association work to keep it healthy.

carnival delights unite with the sounds of barkers on the midway, extolling the virtues of their exhibits; 4-H competitors, grooming their prize animals, are found near the exhibit buildings, where varieties of turkeys, chickens, ducks, and other fowl, unknown to the city dweller, strive for blue ribbons in their respective classes. In the agriculture building, 100-lb. watermelons vie for championships, and pumpkins that a person could not lift charm small children as they think of the upcoming Halloween nights and envision gigantic jack-o'-lanterns. Watching a dairy cow being milked by modern milking machines can captivate an audience of a dozen or two as technology speeds up a chore done by hand by past generations of fairgoers. As night

Now the largest city in Kansas, Wichita, incorporated in 1870, was once an important cattle town. Named for the Wichita Indians who had lived in the south central Kansas area around the Arkansas River, the City has built upon its heritage. The visitor can relive the days of the Old West at Cowtown, the reconstruction of frontier Wichita, enjoy the Mid-American All-Indian Center with the Indian Warrior sculpture "Keeper of the Plains", or drop in on the many museums which help bring its history to life.

Excellent entertainment is available at Century II, the 100,000 square foot facility with concert hall, theater, convention hall and meeting rooms. Symphony, opera, ballet, jazz, country-western, or theatrical performances greet the audience throughout the year. The Wichita Art Museum, Wichita Art Association, and the Ulrich Museum of Art all have fine collections.

This portion of the Wichita skyline from across the river shows Century II and the A. Price Woodard Park.

"Honest, Grandpa, I caught two. The other one was bigger."

The mirrored reflections in Prairie Center Pond are disturbed only occasionally by a splashing fish.

In just a few hours this milk might be in a soft serve cone cooling off a hot visitor to the state fair in Hutchinson.

falls, the color and flurry of the midway take on new life. Glowing ferris wheels, sparkling Viking ships, and shining carrousels create a fairyland. The cares of the world are forgotten as the big-name entertainment begins. The Oak Ridge Boys, Anne Murray, Kenny Rogers, Bob Hope, and many others have been among the famous performers who have appeared in recent years to fill the 10,000-seat grandstand to capacity.

In addition to entertainment and competition, the fair offers trade shows and educational opportunities. A petting zoo and exhibits of farm equipment, cooking, quilting, needlework, and fine arts are also available.

Rodeos offer a different type of competition and entertainment as

These modern wranglers hitch up at the rail.
Theirs is the promise of happy eating at the Sonic.

This Kansas prairie hawk stands a lone vigil above
the mid-winter La Cygne location.

The Sioux Indian word for "People of the South Wind" is Kansas. Pow-wows help celebrate the state's Indian heritage each summer.

cowboys and cowgirls vie for prizes in roping, barrel racing, and riding bucking steeds, while the clowns who rescue downed riders add humor and excitement for the crowd.

Festivals celebrate a wide variety of activities—from maple trees turning color to the Indian pow-wows. Ethnic festivals celebrate the ancestry of Kansans, from the Czech After-Harvest Festival in Wilson, to the Mexican festivals in Topeka and Garden City. In Lindsborg, Swedish festivities are scheduled in odd-numbered years. Neewollah is celebrated in Independence in October. The annual Renaissance Festival, outside Bonner Springs near the grounds of the Agricultural Hall of Fame, brings thousands of Kansans to live vicariously the life of Old England, if only for a day. Liberal has its international pancake race, and Medicine Lodge reenacts the Peace Treaty Pageant, simulating the signing of the treaty between the five tribes and the white man in 1867. In Council Grove, Wah-Shun-Gal Days include an arts and crafts festival as well as a sharing of the historic sites of the region. In Wichita, in May, the Windwagon Parade begins ten days of fun at the annual Wichita River Festival, which includes a symphony concert, sky sports, a bathtub race, and much more. Dozens of other arts and crafts fairs blossom across the state.

Relaxing might also take the form of tracing some of the Kansas heritage. Museums abound throughout the state, commemorating the people and events of long ago. In Sedan, the face of Emmett Kelly, Weary Willie, the clown, looks out to the traveler from paintings and photographs as if to entertain one last time. Reconstructed sites like "Little House on the Prairie" near Independence attract curious visitors. More than two hundred and fifty places are listed on the National Register of Historic Places, and over a dozen National Historic Landmarks are located in Kansas. A summer's

The Renaissance of olden days lives on each year in Wyandotte County near the Agricultural Hall of Fame. Jousters, jugglers and maids-in-waiting abound.

"Standing on Oread hill, by the university, [I] have launch'd my view across broad expanses of living green, in every direction—I have again been most impress'd... with that feature of the topography of your western central world—that vast Something, stretching out on its own unbounded scale, unconfined, which there is in these prairies...."

Walt Whitman

"Rock Chalk, Jayhawk, KU" Panoramic view shows the University of Kansas campus at Lawrence.

"The schools will be open, but the buses will not be running the rural routes today."

Today's Kansans realize that the gold of Coronado's dreams was here—in the golden fields of grain and the flourishing oil fields. Another Kansas treasure is the delight of seasonal change. In a land of four seasons, the golden glow of the sun shines upon green fields and dogwood blossoms in springtime, enriches the ripening grains of summer, flashes on the reds, golds, and oranges of autumn leaves, and shimmers on the blue-white of winter's ice and snow.

For farm land, winter is a time of beauty, peace, and rest. Winter wheat slumbers under the mantel of white, ready to burst forth with spring's green shoots. Ice crystals decorate barbed wire fences with glistening highlights as nature rests. The beauty of each season seems to outdo the last, as winter becomes spring, and summer, fall. Each has its own special virtue.

A part of the Railroad Museum in the depot at Ottawa . . . cool, quiet, unique, with a mixture of the present steeped in history.

One of many architectural gems found in Atchison, Hetherington House is on the National Register of Historic Places.

Not all Kansas cultural events are in theaters, auditoriums and museums. Each Memorial Day weekend the River Bend Art Festival in Atchison brings art and patrons together under the sun.

vacation could be spent searching them out and learning much about the state and its beginnings. Visit any of the forts—Riley, Larned, Scott, Hays, or Leavenworth. Go to Hanover and see the Hollenburg Pony Express Station, still preserved as if awaiting the sound of riders approaching for fresh mounts. Go to the Agricultural Hall of Fame in Bonner Springs, and try to imagine the lives of the early frontier families, or visit during the threshing contest, when they bring the old machines back to life for the day.

Arts and crafts fairs, concerts, horse races, car races, museums and galleries, festivals, rodeos, and fairs add to the choices of the Kansan in summer. All help to celebrate Kansas life. Governor Arthur Capper was right when he said, "Our wandering sons and daughters cannot resist 'the call of Kansas,' but will come back to 'that parallelogram of plenty' we love so well."

Homesteaders on the Santa Fe Trail often stopped in Council Grove at the Post Office Oak to see if a message had been left for them in the hollow of the tree.

The stillness of a new snow adds to the serenity of the hilltop church in winter.

*Kansas is a state of the union, but it is also a state of mind . . .
The barometer of the nation . . .
When anything is going to happen in the country, it happens first in Kansas . . .
Kansas is a spiritual tuning fork."*

William Allen White

The old stone church glows in the afternoon sunlight.

Only three buildings break the solitude of this range land near Hoisington. The center storm cellar was used only rarely, but provided the greatest feeling of security.

A quiet evening in a typical small Kansas town.

Pink blossoms and green leaves signal the return of spring to Kansas.

"Farmhouse in Evening"

All it takes is a little sand and a lot of imagination.

Patriotism bursts forth on the Fourth of July as Kansans from many backgrounds celebrate freedom and independence. Fireworks stands like this one are almost like the vibrant fall colors... full blown one day... gone the next.

Though the setting sun marks the end of another day, tomorrow may bring an unexpected February thaw, an unexpected freeze ... or perhaps a trip to town to compare seed hybrids, buy something for the newest grandbaby, and share a cup of coffee and piece of homemade pie with a friend. All in all ... it's a great life being from the Kansas land.

There's no question that there are some odd customs still continued by today's Kansans. Perhaps this is one way of showing that, even though the boots are worn, the trail continues and the path leads on to tomorrow.

Back end sheets: *"Kaw River Sunset"* south of Bonner Springs.

105